The
ADVENTURES
of
LIL' STEVIE

BOOK 1: CANINES, CAMPOUTS, AND COUSINS

by:
Steve Fitzhugh

TOUCH
PUBLISHING

Copyright © 2013 by Steve Fitzhugh

Author photo by Robert Shanklin

Printed in the United States of America
ISBN: 978-0-9919839-1-9 [print]
ISBN: 978-0-9919839-4-0 [eBook]

Touch Publishing
Requests for publishing / ordering should be directed to:
P.O. Box 180303
Arlington, Texas 76096
www.TouchPublishingServices.com

To schedule Steve Fitzhugh to bring a high-energy, engaging, passionate message to your next event, contact him through his website: www.PowerMoves.org

This book is dedicated to Charles "Chucky" Fitzhugh. You brought priceless memories and loads of laughter to my childhood. Every child deserves to have a big brother like you. Thank you!

Contents

Introduction

Little Stevie Fitzhugh - *that's fits-you, fits-me, fits-everybody* - was the fourth-born child to Eva and Ray Fitzhugh. Stevie came along on January 28, 1963. Since his father Ray was the baby of *his* family, Lil' Stevie was often referred to as the "baby's baby." He knew this because when his grandma on his father's side visited, she'd wrap her large, loving arms around him and affectionately say, "<u>You</u> are the baby's baby." She had a soft spot for Stevie that was obvious to everyone. You could even say she spoiled him (though all of her grand-babies were special).

She always told Stevie, "One day I'm gonna take you wherever you wanna go!"

Lil' Stevie dreamed about that promised day. He would remember the names of interesting places he saw on television, or that he read about in books, so he could tell Grandma Angeline where he wanted to go, if and when that special day came. It was her promise that made Lil' Stevie want to explore the world, and that desire stayed with him for his entire life.

Stevie lived with his mom, his sister, and two

brothers. His sister's name was Greta; she was the oldest. As a teenager, Greta had lots of friends, a huge afro, and was very pretty.

Raymond, the next oldest, was a terrific athlete and did well in school, too. One day, while sitting at the kitchen table, Stevie looked on in awe while Raymond took a wristwatch completely apart and then put it all back together! Stevie thought Raymond could do anything.

Chucky was three years older than Stevie, and because of how close they were in age, Stevie and Chucky hung out together the most.

Stevie saw his parents' marriage end in divorce before he was seven. Even though things were difficult for Stevie, he had many memorable childhood events. Some of these events led to life-long lessons, others made long-time memories, and yet others can just be chalked up as weird and wacky things that happened.

Stevie's mom had a great sense of humor and was a practical joker. Chucky took after her, and he was the funniest brother ever. He made everyone laugh out loud until their sides hurt. Chucky could make you laugh the kind of laugh that ended up with you begging him to stop being funny so you could catch your breath. It was what Stevie appreciated the most about Chucky. Stevie needed that kind of laughter to break up the sad times. No one wants to see his or her parents get divorced. It was painful.

His parents originally planned for Lil' Stevie's

dad to go to college while his mom stayed home. Then, after he earned his degree, Mom would go to college while Dad worked. Instead, Dad went to college while Mom had one, then two, then three, and then four babies. After that, she had to stay at home while Dad continued in school. He earned another degree, but their relationship fell apart as they grew in separate directions. Their split came with arguments that Stevie didn't understand, and with uninvited pain that hung around Stevie's heart for much too long.

All families have problems. The ones that have the tools and resources to solve those problems succeed. The families that don't know how to solve their problems become what the professionals call: dysfunctional. Lil' Stevie grew up with a lot of dysfunction that he learned to parade as normal in order to move along and get along.

This is the backdrop for *The Adventures of Lil' Stevie*. These are indeed adventures because life itself is an adventure filled with unique experiences, interesting characters, and strange places. Did you know your life is an adventure? It is an adventure which includes highs and lows, joys and sorrows, tears and laughter, all of which provide the tapestry for a story that can only be told by you. You are your life's main character! And in these particular adventures, you'll experience the true stories of Lil' Stevie Fitzhugh - that's *fits-you, fits-me, fits-everybody*!

The Adventures of Lil' Stevie

The Mighty

Invasion of the Squirrels

Growing up on the West Side of Akron, Ohio was a good thing. No, really, it was! Someone else might not think so, but when what you have is all you've known, you are not aware that it could be better.

Stevie's house was special for two reasons. First, there was a hill in the backyard which was great for sledding in the winter. Second, it not only had a cherry tree, it also had three huge apple trees. The big apple trees were excellent for providing both a handy summer snack when one had been playing outside all day, and ample ammunition for apple fights with friends.

Although Stevie had friends who lived on his street and on the next street over, Stevie often played alone. He had a great imagination, which is a must-have if you are playing by yourself and you want to enjoy it! The backyard was the scene of many great adventures.

One perfect summer day, the backyard was host to one such great adventure for Stevie. On that day, the backyard transformed into a kingdom that could only be protected by its champion: Lil' Stevie. The squirrels were on a mission to overtake the kingdom. They filled the trees, ran along branches, trampled the broken swing, and even used the high electric wires to access the rooftops of the royal house and garage. The entire kingdom depended on Stevie, its champion, to thwart the invasion.

A warrior of few weapons, Stevie depended entirely upon apples to defend the Fitzhugh Kingdom Matriarch, the Honorable Queen Eva. Stevie knew that to stop the advance of the troops, he couldn't just hit any squirrel with his apples, he had to hit the *captain* squirrel. If Stevie could get into position, hit the captain with an apple, and escape to the front yard without being attacked by the other squirrels, the kingdom would be saved.

Stevie entered the backyard quietly from the side of the house closest to The Ferrells (his next-door neighbors). The squirrels quickly noticed Mighty Champion Stevie. His reputation preceded him. He was well-known throughout the land as a fearsome conqueror. His apple-throwing skills were unmatched. He was quick and agile. He could hide behind any tree, step out, and, in a split-second, zip an apple twenty feet toward a target with remarkable accuracy.

Lil' Stevie prepared for the epic battle. He loaded up with apples, dashing around the backyard to gather them and returning to the patio to store his ammunition. Looking into the trees, it was clear why he had been summoned. Squirrels were EVERYWHERE! The kingdom was most definitely under attack. Stevie began to hurl apples into the trees in an attempt to identify the captain squirrel. The captain squirrel would be easy to find, he was always the squirrel that went the highest into the trees when under attack.

Zip! Went one apple into the trees.

Zip, Zip! Went two more.

Lil' Stevie was on fire! He hurled apple after apple, non-stop. Squirrels scrambled everywhere trying to evade the young champion appointed to defend the kingdom.

The patio provided Stevie with excellent position. He could see the entire backyard *and* throw downhill at the squirrels on the ground, or straight ahead to squirrels in the trees.

Then it happened! The captain squirrel emerged above the other squirrels in the highest tree, on the highest branch. His thick, bushy tail curled waaaaay upward and seemed as large as a fox's tail! He stared down at Stevie, and Stevie stared back. Then, as quickly as he was identified, he took off down the branch, leaping out of sight, bouncing from one branch to the next.

Zip, Zip! Stevie launched apples into the air. *Zip, Zip!* He didn't quit. The battle waged on. Stevie continued to reposition himself to get a better angle at the captain squirrel. He could feel his heart pumping hard. It was thrilling.

His throws, however, continued to land short of the prized target. The kingdom was about to fall. Queen Eva was in peril. Near desperation, Stevie committed to do something that had never been done before. It was dangerous and definitely scary. Stevie surveyed the yard and formed the risky plan. If he left the safety of the patio, went down into the backyard and crouched beneath the trees, he could get a better shot at the captain. Of course, this would mean he would be exposed to the bandit squirrels and vulnerable to their attack. But he *had* to do it, there was no time to wait. His kingdom was in jeopardy.

His heart pounded even stronger as he grabbed as many apples as his small hands could carry and tentatively descended the patio. The champion slowly walked down the hill. When he reached the point that he felt was as far as he could go without falling prey to the fierce invaders, he stopped. But there was no captain.

"Where did he go?" Stevie asked aloud.

The minion squirrels lurked about, but the bushy-tailed captain was nowhere in sight. It wasn't easy to turn in a circle with an armload of apples while scanning the trees above, but Stevie was desperate to save the kingdom. He concentrated hard on finding the captain. Stevie took a step, not realizing his back was now only a few feet from the largest tree. Then, without warning, from the other side of the trunk of that giant tree, the captain jumped out!

Stevie was face-to-face with the enemy. Time froze for a moment as Stevie's big brown eyes looked into the captain's small black ones. Terror and panic swelled inside, and Stevie dropped all of his apples as he ran back up the hill as fast as his legs could go. It wasn't until he was safely at the patio that he realized the captain wasn't chasing him.

Catching his breath and turning, Stevie realized the captain was perched on a low branch, out in the open.

"What a perfect place. I know I can hit him from here!" Stevie said.

He grabbed an apple from the patio stockpile. He faced the captain, who obviously thought he was safely out of the champion's reach. With his heart nearly bursting from his chest, Stevie took his most careful aim.

Zip! Stevie whipped the apple at the unsuspecting captain.

The thud was unmistakable. It was a direct hit! Stevie's apple smacked the captain squirrel on his side. Stevie's eyes widened in horror as he watched the captain's small body fall to the ground. The captain paused a moment, obviously in pain and out of breath. Then he quickly scampered away.

Stevie stood there. The battle was over. The kingdom was saved. He should feel elated! But he didn't. Stevie didn't feel happy at all with his accomplishment. The reality that this little game actually hurt an innocent squirrel made Lil' Stevie sad.

The sound of the thud that the apple made against the squirrel's body echoed in Stevie's ears. It was no longer imagination, but real life. He replayed the scene in his mind and watched the poor squirrel leave the backyard.

Stevie thought about the time that a bully came up to him on the school playground and punched him for no reason. He thought about how mad he was because he didn't deserve it. He was sure the squirrel felt the same way. He didn't deserve it either.

That was the last time Lil' Stevie would ever throw apples at a squirrel, or hurt any animal, because he didn't want anyone to hurt him. Sometimes you might do something without thinking about the consequences. Sometimes you might say hurtful things without thinking how your words will affect another. Whatever good reason you think you may have for saying things that bring pain, at the end of the matter, it's simply not worth it.

Camping Out

One day Stevie overheard his big brother Chucky making plans with Jeffrey Tate, the teenager next door, for an overnight campout in Stevie's backyard. It was a hot day in July, sweltering actually, near the middle of summer vacation. Camping out was a great idea because without air conditioning, the house was always hot at night. Outside, it was much cooler. Even with the windows open, fans blowing full-throttle, and sleeping with your pajama top off, it was hard to get a good night's sleep in the heat.

"Chucky, you guys gonna really camp out tonight?" he asked.

"Yeah, Stevie, just me an' Jeff," responded Chucky.

"Can I camp too?" Stevie asked. "I can help build the tent and I'll even guard it?" he pleaded.

"No Stevie, it's going to be me and Jeff. No little kids allowed," Chucky declared.

Being the baby of the family occasionally had its

privileges. Stevie didn't use his "baby of the family" trump card all the time, but when there was something he *really* wanted, he would go to his mom and state his case wearing the saddest eyes he could muster.

This was one of those times. He just *had* to camp out with Chucky and Jeff, and only Mom could make that call. It would be so much fun, even if there were no other kids his age. Chucky and Jeff had their own reasons for not wanting Lil' Stevie around, but Stevie didn't know this when he begged his momma to overturn the bigger boys' decision.

"Mom, Chucky and Jeff are going to make a tent and camp outside tonight. Chucky said I can't be with them because it's just going to be big kids. Can I please, please, PLEASE camp out tonight? I don't have anybody to play with, and it's going to be soooooo hot in the house. Mom, can I please?" Lil' Stevie pleaded his most powerful plea and crossed his fingers.

Mom gave in quickly. "Chucky, you and Jeff let Stevie camp with you guys tonight. You know he doesn't have anybody his age to play with!" Mom ordered.

"Awe, Mom … Stevie's going to be in the way!" Chucky defended.

"What did I say?" Mom stood her ground. For Chucky and Jeff it was either camp with Stevie or no camping at all.

"All right, Stevie, you can camp with us," Chucky conceded. Then he added adamantly, "But you have to do whatever I tell you to do!"

They didn't have real tents. They tossed blankets over the old, A-frame swing set in the backyard and, using a heavy brick, they hammered broken sticks through the blankets and into the ground to secure them. Of course for Chucky and Jeff it was just a tent. But to Stevie it was so much more! It was a clubhouse, a hide-away, a fort! He was going to have so much fun, he could barely stand it.

Outside the tent, Chucky began to dig a hole for the campfire. He sent Stevie to gather as many sticks and twigs as possible to fuel it. Gathering sticks wasn't a real exciting job, but it didn't matter. The fact that Stevie was actually camping outside for the first time with his big brother was reason enough to do whatever Chucky asked.

It was just starting to get dark. Stevie couldn't wait to start the fire. They really didn't need a campfire, but Chucky said having a fire made the campsite official. Backyard camping is super-convenient. If you have to use the bathroom, all you have to do is go up the hill to the house. And, you don't need to worry about cooking food, because Mom makes you eat dinner inside before you head out for the night.

So with full stomachs, darkness all around, and a small campfire burning, it was finally time for the guys to hang out at the campsite and just be guys. Jeff and Chucky talked about teenager stuff while Stevie added sticks to the fire. Keeping the fire going was Stevie's job. Chucky thought Stevie didn't realize that his fire assignment was a ploy to keep him out of the tent so he and Jeff could talk about big-kid stuff. Of course, Stevie knew what was going on. But it didn't matter because, once again, Stevie was just glad to be out there.

It was getting late. Staring into the campfire for so long made Lil' Stevie very sleepy. He could hear Chucky and Jeff planning something, but they talked quietly so Stevie wouldn't hear. They emerged from the tent and Stevie perked up.

"Stevie, me and Jeff are gonna go for walk. You stay here and guard the fire and don't let it go out until we get back," Chucky ordered.

"You want me to stay in this backyard by myself?" Stevie repeated.

"Be a big boy, Stevie and don't be scared. We'll be right back," Chucky insisted.

"Chucky, it's almost eleven o'clock! You gonna get in trouble if you break curfew," Stevie warned.

In Akron, Ohio there was an eleven o'clock curfew during the summer for children under eighteen-years-old. Lawbreakers were punished. Local television stations announced the curfew regularly: "It's eleven o'clock, do you know where your children are?" It was never an issue for Stevie because there was no way he would ever break a law.

"Stevie, just stay here and watch the fire," Chucky said with exasperation.

Stevie made up his mind right then that there was

no way he was going to stay alone in this big, dark backyard all by himself while Chucky and Jeff took a walk. As soon as Chucky and Jeff ascended the hill, passed the patio, and made their way to the front of the house, Stevie chased after them. Trying his best to stay out of sight, Stevie followed at a safe distance as they walked down the street.

Stevie soon realized this was no, "I'll be right back" kind of walk. They were going far. By now it was well after eleven and the farther they went, the more afraid Stevie grew. There was no way he could turn back alone. Stevie began to imagine what would happen when they were caught by the police. He pictured what it would be like to be hauled off to jail for breaking curfew. Stevie's eyes were as big as saucers and he strained to see Jeff and Chucky now. He knew he had to catch up and turn himself in to his big brother. He also knew Chucky would be mad, but at least he wouldn't be alone.

"Chucky wait up!" Stevie cried out into the night with a squeaky voice that dripped with fear.

"Stevie, is that you?" Chucky yelled back, with obvious disappointment.

"Yeah, Chuck, it's me! The fire went out so I decided to catch up with you guys," Stevie said trying to justify his defiance of his given orders. "Where you guys going?"

"C'mon Stevie, we're going to Krispy Kreme. Stay close to us and walk in the shadows of the streetlights when you see a car coming. If it's the police, we gonna run!" Chucky instructed angrily.

Krispy Kreme had the best donuts in town and were open 24 hours a day! What a treat. Stevie thought dreamily.

Stevie couldn't believe Jeff and Chucky tried to deprive him of such a remarkable delight. Krispy Kreme donuts! All kinds of questions swirled in Lil' Stevie's head.

Where did they get the money for the donuts? Did they have enough for him? What if they get caught? These concerns made Stevie uneasy. His only peace came from the fact that Chucky and Jeff appeared to have no problem at all with what was going on.

There was enough change for each of them to have one milk and one donut. Stevie was delighted. Krispy Kreme glazed donuts and milk were almost like heaven. He would have enjoyed it more had it not been past curfew. They made it there safely without being noticed by the police. Now they needed to make the return trip.

Although Krispy Kreme was only a mile and a half down Copley Road, it could have been twenty miles away as far as Stevie was concerned. His legs, much smaller than Chucky's and Jeff's, made it difficult to keep up. He worked twice as hard to move just as fast as they were going. He didn't want to ask them to slow down. He wanted to prove he could hang with the big boys. Halfway home and so far without a hitch, Jeff noticed a grocery cart from the nearby grocery store abandoned on the side of the road.

"Hold up Chuck, I'm gonna go get that cart!" Jeff announced.

"Okay Tate, I'll get in it and you can push," Chucky suggested.

"Noooo!" Stevie shouted. "It's too loud, we're gonna get in trouble!" Stevie pleaded, but his beckoning fell on deaf ears.

Sure enough, Jeff Tate grabbed the grocery cart, Chucky jumped in, and the two of them raced down Copley Road making all kinds of noise, AFTER CURFEW! They hadn't gone one full block when the next car that came down the street was a POLICE CAR!

"STEVIE, RUN!" Chucky shouted.

Chucky fell out of the cart and he and Jeff bolted down a side street. Stevie followed faster than he'd ever run before. Taking Jeff's lead, all three boys sat on the porch of the first house they came to. The police cruiser, having made a u-turn with wheels screeching, soon came down the street. He shone his flood light on the three under-aged boys, sitting casually on the porch, and he began his questioning.

"Do you boys live here?" he asked.

"Yes sir," Jeff responded without hesitation.

"What are you boys doing out after curfew?" the officer queried.

Stevie could actually hear his heart pounding in

his ears, and he was certain the officer could hear it, too. All of the sudden, camping out wasn't so important to him. Running with the big boys wasn't important either. All Stevie could think about was being home in his bed, asleep where he was supposed to be. At this point he was certain that he was headed to jail, his name would be in the newspaper, and there would be no more of Mom's delicious fried chicken. In the Fitzhugh house, if you did something that was so bad your name got put in the paper, there was no future for you.

"I need one of you boys to go inside and get your mom to come to the door," the officer instructed.

"Okay, we'll go get her. We don't have our key so we'll have to go in the back door," Chucky said.

He also quietly whispered through tight lips, "As soon as we get to the back, run for your life!"

You'll get no argument from me, Stevie thought to himself.

The boys slowly walked to the back of the unknown residence and, as soon as they were out of the sight of the cruiser, they ran all the way home like there was no tomorrow. They jumped fences, cut through backyards, went through branches, and ducked trees until they ended up at 1082 Roslyn Avenue and safely at the campsite. Jeff was bleeding from a sticker bush he ran through, and Chucky was laughing out loud.

"What's so funny Chucky?" Stevie asked, still breathing heavy from the run.

"When we were running I looked back at you and

all I could see were your eyes! I saw your head but no mouth or nose, just two, big, scared-to-death eyes!" Chucky blurted in between gales of laughter.

"Fitz-Al, When I looked back, your legs were moving so fast I couldn't even see 'em in the dark. I thought you were flyin'!" Jeff added with a chuckle that only made Chucky laugh harder. Fitz-Al is what Jeff called Stevie. It was his own made-up term of endearment that was a combination of the first half of Fitzhugh and an abbreviation of Stevie's middle name, Allen.

Stevie learned a lesson that night. Not every <u>thing</u> is for every <u>body</u>. Running with a bigger, older crowd doesn't make you any bigger or older, and might get you in a predicament that you aren't ready for. Stevie realized it's probably best to associate with friends his own age. And even then, have the courage to say "no" to what you know is not right. When you take risks and put yourself in danger, you put your future on the line and your destination may not be where you wanted to go.

The Adventures of Lil' Stevie

Poochie
Goes to Practice

It's a fact of life that when you have athletic brothers, whether you want to or not, everyone will expect *you* to play sports, too. Lucky for Stevie he liked sports just as much as his brothers did. Raymond was especially good in all sports. He was fast, strong, skilled, and smart. He played football, basketball, baseball, and even ran track.

Chucky was good, too. He wasn't as big in size as Raymond, but that didn't matter. Chucky excelled in basketball and baseball. He could bat right and left-handed, and when he was up at bat, he was particularly good at placing the ball anywhere he wanted. It amazed people how Chucky could drop the ball wherever the coach told him. He was the lead-off batter and always got on base.

Just like his brothers, Stevie played Pee Wee Football and Farm League Baseball. Stevie had fun playing baseball. When he started playing, he didn't always get in the game, but his game time increased the more he learned how to play.

Having Chucky around was a big plus for Stevie. Chucky played catch with Stevie and taught him how to throw a curve ball. He would walk Stevie all the way down to Maple Valley Field where practices and games were held. The day the uniforms were given out, Stevie came home and had to ask Chucky how to put on those crazy-looking socks. Yes, having Chucky was a big plus for Stevie.

Raymond had a dog named Poochie. They called him Pooh for short. Pooh was a short-haired cocker-beagle. Occasionally Raymond would try and teach Pooh to be an attack-dog, but sweet Pooh didn't have it in him. He was simply a nice dog. One day, when Chucky wasn't around to play catch with him, Stevie said to himself: *I need to practice throwing and catching, but there's no one to throw the ball back to me.* He was sitting on the front porch, petting Pooh and wondering how he could practice without Chucky. Stevie thought long and hard about what to do.

"I got it!" he said out loud. "I'll use Pooh!"

Although Poochie was Raymond's dog, Stevie was his caretaker. He fed Pooh, played with Pooh, walked Pooh, and even taught Pooh a few tricks.

Stevie grabbed his baseball glove and his ball. He didn't have a real baseball, so he used a tennis ball. Chucky always used the tennis ball so he wouldn't hurt Stevie's hand when he threw it real hard. Stevie turned to Pooh and made a ticking sound by sucking air through the side of his mouth and clicking his tongue against his teeth. Pooh knew that was his cue to get up and follow Lil' Stevie.

Stevie ran with Pooh jumping at his heels. Stevie showed Pooh the yellow tennis ball and then, winding up like a pitcher, Stevie threw the ball down the street. Pooh ran after the ball as if he had been shot from a cannon. He tracked it down, snatched it up into his mouth, and returned lickety-split to Stevie. Stevie repeated his pitching motions again before firing another fastball pitch as far as he could down the street. Again, Pooh retrieved the ball. After a few more tries, this ordeal got to be pretty boring for Pooh. On his next retrieval, he ran past Stevie and made Stevie chase him for the ball. Pooh ran down the street with Stevie in hot pursuit.

"POOH!" Stevie shouted in an attempt to slow down the canine.

Pooh ran into the neighbor's yard, waited on Stevie to catch up, and bolted off again. The ball was still in Pooh's mouth when Stevie gave out due to exhaustion. Pooh, seeing that Stevie was done with the game of chase, trotted over to Stevie and dropped the ball in front of him. The wag of his tail seemed to ask, "Are we still friends?"

Stevie had so much fun with Pooh he decided to bring him to baseball practice. It seemed like a great idea.

"Stevie, if you are gonna take Pooh with you, make sure you have him on a leash," Mom instructed. "And make sure you tie him up good while you are on the field!"

"I will, Mom," Stevie promised.

There were two ways to get to Maple Valley Field from 1082 Roslyn Avenue. You could either go to the first corner, Lawton Street, make a left, take the next right at Orlando Avenue, and walk to the field in cool shade. Or you could simply go all the way down Roslyn Avenue and make a left at the field. The problem with the second route was that it kept you in the hot sun. The shady road was definitely preferred, but it had a problem. Diablo! Stevie was even scared of that name, D-I-A-B-L-O!

Diablo was a huge, white St. Bernard dog that was the spitting image of a polar bear. He lived at the corner of Lawton and Orlando. If Diablo broke his chain (which he did at least once a week), Stevie was certain to become Diablo's dinner and Pooh would be dessert. Stevie decided to take the sunny route down Roslyn.

That day, it seemed like every dog on Roslyn Avenue had something to say to Pooh. As they passed from house to house, if there was a dog in the yard, it was barking.

"What's going on around here?" Stevie asked Pooh. "Can't a little boy walk his dog in peace?"

Pooh didn't answer. Stevie began to rehearse all

the things his mom said not to do if a dog approached him.

"Do not run!" he heard her say.

That doesn't make much sense. Should I just stand there and be eaten? He mused over this question. Stevie and Pooh were almost to the final corner, when a medium-sized dog with wild eyes ran toward them. Forgetting Mom's words of wisdom, Stevie dropped Pooh's leash and ran. He ran like lightning! The dog chased Stevie to the corner where he ran around parked cars, screaming in horror. He was sure he was being chased by a flesh-eating monster. Stevie quickly ran out of options. Mild-mannered Pooh looked on, but was no help to Stevie and seemed unlikely to get involved in this mess, even though he started the whole thing. Suddenly the dog stopped running. Stevie stopped too. The only thing between them was a telephone pole. The pause in chase was only for a second, but it seemed like an eternity. Then, in what seemed like slow motion, the dog made his move around the pole. Stevie turned to run, but he was not fast enough. The dog lunged at Stevie and sunk his teeth right into Stevie's back! After the chomp, the dog ran away. It hurt. A lady had seen the whole ordeal from her porch, and she came to Stevie's aid to inspect the bite.

"Don't look like that ole' mangy dog did any damage boy," she said in a raspy voice. "He barely broke the skin on ya back. Go on home n' let ya momma look at it more betta."

Stevie sobbed. Not entirely because of the pain, but because the thought of having been bitten by a dog was overwhelming. One of the things he feared most in life had really happened. And you know what? Although it was a scary thing, it wasn't all that bad. Stevie reflected on this thought as he wandered back home. When he got there, Mom confirmed that the skin was barely broken and nothing to worry about. Then she babied Stevie with some tender loving care. It was more like a scratch than a bite. From that day on, Pooh stayed home when Stevie went to practice.

It's amazing how paralyzing fear can be. Maybe Stevie was not supposed to run, but he ran anyway. It would be interesting to see how that day would have ended had Stevie confronted his fears instead of running from them. Maybe the dog would have been the one being chased and not Stevie? It turned out that this fear had a big bark, but a tiny bite. When you are afraid, you should follow the wisdom given to you by your parents or trusted teachers. If you can't think of a good solution, then confront your fear and remember that most of the time, whatever you are afraid of won't be as bad as you think.

Strike Out

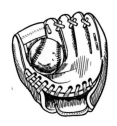

The Fitzhugh name was relatively well-known in the community, thanks to the sports skills of Stevie's brothers. Raymond was easily the fastest on the block and Chucky could "shake and bake" anyone on the basketball court. The older Fitzhugh brothers were always the first to be chosen in any pick-up game of basketball or friendly football competition.

And then there was Lil' Stevie.

Lil' Stevie Fitzhugh had yet to prove himself athletically. He wasn't as aggressive as his brothers when it came to sports. He liked to play, but could be just as happy going to the library and reading a book. Stevie's enrollment in sports teams was more by default than intention. He was *expected* to sign up for baseball and football - and that expectation landed Stevie on the team.

One thing Lil' Stevie did possess was speed. During recess in the second grade, Stevie could out-run all of the girls and almost all of the boys on the playground. This really helped his odds when he tried out for the neighborhood baseball team. Of course, since there was not a large pool of kids to pick from, the coaches pretty much allowed everyone to make the team, but because of Stevie's speed and success catching the ball, Stevie was assigned to play center field. Playing catch with Chucky all the time helped Stevie develop excellent catching skills. Throwing the ball all the way to the corner so Pooh could fetch it made Stevie's arm strong. Playing center field was perfect!

Batting, however, was a different story. Stevie didn't have the same access to developing batting skills as he did with running, throwing, and catching. First, you need to have a bat in order to practice, which the Fitzhugh boys did not. Second, you need several baseballs. Stevie and his brothers only had one hard ball, the rest were tennis balls. You also need someone to field the balls and throw them back to the pitcher. This wasn't something Stevie could do on his own, or even with Pooh. Without these necessities, batting practice was a wash, and so Stevie's only batting practice happened with his team. Even then, Stevie wasn't guaranteed to get coaching help with his batting because his coach had a full-time job. Some weeks, Coach could only stay for part of the practice and sometimes he couldn't come at all.

As a result, Stevie rarely swung at the ball when he was at bat in a game. The fact of the matter was that because he didn't practice it much, Stevie was afraid to swing. The pitches came fast and hard and were not very accurate. Fortunately, the pitchers' skill levels were low enough to assure that Stevie got on base with a walk most of the time by simply *not* swinging. Once there, he could use his speed to steal bases and, if the next batter got a hit, Stevie could run fast enough to score every time.

One day, Stevie's team was up against the league's best team. The pitcher was one of the most feared in the league, Dooley Williams. Dooley could do something no other pitcher in the Little League could do, he could throw a *curve ball*! Most pitchers just tried to get the ball over the plate, never mind trying to do anything special with it. But Dooley's father, who was also a coach, taught Dooley how to throw a curve ball!

Statistics show the difference between the skill levels of young athletes is predicated on the amount of extra practice time a young athlete gets with his or her father. After his parents' divorce, Stevie didn't see his father much, nor did his dad work with him to give him extra practice. If it had not been for Chucky, Stevie would have been even further behind the other kids than he was. In order to win this game, Stevie's team needed hits, not walks! Besides, Dooley didn't walk many batters.

"Fitzhugh on deck!" Stevie's coached yelled before Stevie's first at-bat.

Stevie felt the pressure to perform, and he was

nervous. The average crowd (a few parents and a handful of random passer-bys) was gathered. Stevie stood in the on-deck circle and took a few warm-up swings. Stevie's custom was to swing two bats at a time for practice. Chucky had taught him that, saying it would make the bat feel lighter when you got to the plate. To Stevie it didn't matter whether the bat was heavy or light, because he had no intention of swinging.

Crack! Big D, Stevie's teammate, hit the ball. Everyone cheered him on, even Stevie.

"Run D, run! Go, go, go!" Stevie shouted. Big D landed a solid base hit that he stretched into a double.

"Stevie, keep it going! Another hit and we can get on the board," informed the coach, excitedly.

Stevie grabbed his helmet and headed to the batter's box. His mouth was dry, his heart pounded, and a part of him just wanted this moment over.

"Batter up!" yelled the umpire.

Stevie stepped into position. He rehearsed all of Chucky's instructions. "Feet shoulder length apart … bend your knees … bat straight up and keep it still … right elbow high … watch the ball not the pitcher … "

"THE PITCHER!" Stevie gasped on the inside. In the excitement of Big D's hit, he'd almost forgotten about Dooley! *Woosh-peesh!* The pitch flew by, sticking in the catcher's mitt with a thud!

"Strike one!" yelled the umpire. Then the ump added, "Whaaat? Lil' Fitzhugh caught looking?"

Stevie then noticed that the umpire was one of his

brother Raymond's good friends from Roslyn Avenue.

Oh Great! Stevie thought to himself. *Will Daniels, better known as Still Will, is going to give Raymond a play-by-play account of everything I do today.*

"C'mon Stevie, give it a good swing! You can do it!" coached Stevie's teammates.

Woosh-peesh!

"BALL!" shouted the ump.

Phew! Stevie thought. Good thing it was a ball. Stevie didn't even see the pitch! Stevie stared at the mound, waiting for Dooley's next pitch. Stevie heard about this famous curve ball but had never seen one before.

Woosh-peesh! Dooley threw a fastball, high and inside. The ball headed right at Stevie's chin. He jumped back just in time, escaping what could've been a very painful experience.

"BALL TWO!" shouted Still Will the umpire.

One strike, two balls. A walk was looking better and better. Two more balls and he'd be on base.

"Good eye, Stevie! Good eye!" the coach shouted.

Stevie liked to hear his coach say that. It made him feel he was doing something right. He knew what coach meant. Stevie didn't think of it as having a good eye, he was just scared to death to get hit. He didn't want that fastball to bust him in the head. Before he had time to think about the next pitch, Dooley was already in his wind-up pitching motion.

Woosh-peesh! Dooley released another fastball and it was coming full speed right at Lil' Stevie's head. (Or so it seemed.) Just like before, Stevie jumped back in the nick of time. But this time, the ball dropped and curved right into the strike zone and smacked into the catcher's glove.

"STRIIIIIIIIKE!" yelled the umpire. "Oh my, a Fitzhugh jumping back from a strike?"

That was a strike? Stevie thought in surprise. If Stevie had never seen a curve ball before, he sure knew what one looked like now. Dooley had Stevie right where he wanted him. Stevie didn't know what pitch to expect next. It didn't really matter, because whether it was a curve ball, fastball, or slider, Stevie wasn't going to swing. He was waiting on that walk. Dooley was pitching from the stretch now instead of the wind-up. He wanted to make sure Big D couldn't get a lead off but kept close to second base. There were two outs, and Dooley knew he had to get Lil' Stevie out.

Woosh-peesh! "BALL THREE!" called the umpire. "The count is full!"

Stevie knew from Chucky's teaching that a full count means there are two strikes and three balls. The next pitch will force either a strikeout or walk if there is no hit.

"Good eye, Stevie, good eye!" the coach complimented.

Maybe I do have a good eye. Maybe my coach is

right. Maybe the people with good eyes get the hits. All I have to do is swing, Stevie coached himself. Big D was at second, there were two outs, Dooley was on the mound, and Stevie was at bat.

"All right, Fitzhugh. Whutcha gonna do?" Still Will said, in a sing-song rhythm. Dooley was already in the stretch.

"Hey batter, batter, hey batter, batter!" chanted the infield.

Dooley released the pitch. It was a hot one! Big D took off running. Stevie saw the ball this time. He actually saw the ball coming. It was definitely going to be a strike. He knew because he had his good eye on it. All he had to do was swing! And swing he did! He raised his elbow, lifted his front leg to step into the swing. And with all his might Stevie swung the bat. It was happening in slow motion for Stevie.

Whiffff! Stevie missed. It was a fastball right down the pipe.

"BATTERRRRR'S OOOOOUT!" screamed the umpire.

"Stevie, never close your eyes," he heard Chucky's instructions in his head. It was a good pitch, it was a great swing, but Stevie closed his eyes at the last moment and missed the ball.

"That's all right Stevie. You can get 'em next time!" the coach encouraged.

Stevie didn't even want to look into the eyes of any of his teammates because he felt he had let them down.

"It's early in the game buddy," Big D said as he headed to the mound. "Keep ya' head up!"

Stevie struck out again. But Dooley was striking everybody out. Fastball, curve ball, fastball, curve ball. The good thing was that Big D (who also pitched for Stevie's team) was striking out kids, too. In the bottom of the last inning, Stevie got another chance. With no outs, Big D hit a home run. There was no fence at the Maple Valley field, so if you hit the ball all the way to Hawkins Avenue, it was an automatic home run. Big D's homer tied the game at one to one. There were no outs, so the pressure was off Lil' Stevie. If he struck out for the third time, the team would still have two outs to go. The pressure would be on someone else. Stevie came to the batter's box. He wasn't afraid of Dooley. Strange enough, he wasn't even afraid to swing.

Woosh-peesh!

"CRACK!" Stevie swung as hard as he could at the first pitch, with HIS EYES OPEN! He connected on a screamer. He was so stunned he almost forgot to run. As he rounded first base and headed to second, he looked back at Still Will but didn't understand the helicopter swirling motion he was making above his head with his hand.

"HOMERUN!" the ump declared.

Stevie's ball was long and deep and hit the roof of the equipment shed at the edge of the third base line in left field. That was an automatic homerun. The game was over! Stevie was overjoyed as he continued to circle the bases for his homerun.

Stevie proved to himself that day that just because you don't get it right the first time, doesn't mean that you stop trying. He was in the same batter's box, with the same pitcher throwing to him, in the very same game that had made him so nervous earlier. But he realized that if he simply tried again, maybe it would be better. And it was! Every day you have the choice whether or not you are going to try and get better at the things you do. If you do nothing, things won't change. Make up your mind each morning when you wake up that you will keep getting better. Even though it might seem to get worse before it improves, don't quit. The next time it's your turn to bat, take your swing, and keep your eyes open!

The Adventures of Lil' Stevie

Razzle Dazzles

Schumacher Elementary School was only one block away from Stevie's home. Some kids dreaded school, some missed school frequently, and some even played sick in order to stay home from school. That was not the case with Lil' Stevie. He loved school! At the end of the school year, Stevie often received perfect attendance awards. School was an oasis for Stevie. Home was special to him, but in a different kind of way. The happy parts at home were all too often broken up with arguments. Smiles became tears, and there was too much sadness, anger, and, at times, violence. Perfect attendance was partly about Stevie's love for school, but it also was his escape from dysfunction at home.

Although Stevie's parents were not together, his mom still called his dad to come over and discipline the boys when they were disobedient. In other words, Dad did the spanking. One time Chucky got in big trouble. Stevie's mom called his dad to come over and dish out the punishment. Chucky overheard Mom making the request on the phone. Knowing Dad was on the way,

Chucky put on five pairs of pants in preparation of his whipping. When Dad arrived, Chucky had on so many pairs of pants he could barely move. Their dad quickly recognized that Chucky had dramatically "gained a little weight" since last they saw each other and Chucky's padded plot was uncovered. (Chucky still got a whipping, but it wasn't as bad as it could have been because their dad was laughing so hard he could barely swing the belt.)

As if the spanking wasn't bad enough, usually afterward Stevie's mom and dad always found something to fight about. That part was hard for the kids to understand.

But as for school? School was fun and Stevie enjoyed every minute of it. Of course he always had to be on the lookout for the bullies, but if you could stay away from the mean kids and do what the teacher instructed, school was a piece of cake.

Since the divorce, Stevie's family was on welfare. Stevie and Chucky were on the school-assisted lunch program. Lunchtime was one of Stevie's favorite periods. When the cupboards were bare at home and there was no breakfast to be had, Stevie knew he could rely on school lunch. It was there every day and it was always good. Stevie never understood why so many kids complained about the lunch. The food was hot, different, and even included a dessert!

One day Stevie won a prize in the lunchroom for helping the cafeteria staff clean tables. It was a pack of

Razzles! Razzles were one of Stevie's favorite candies. It started out as a candy, but once you began to chew on it, the candy turned into bubble gum. Many of the other student helpers had hoped to be selected for the prize, but it was Lil' Stevie who won. At Schumacher, you were not allowed to have candy in class, so Stevie forced the package of Razzles into the front pocket on his pants and secured it there, saving them for after school. But one of the school's bullies had his eye on the candy and was determined to take it from Stevie.

"GIVE ME THAT CANDY BOY!" demanded Vernon. Vernon was a fifth-grader known for being mean to younger students. Stevie was in grade three at the time, and any smart third-grader avoided him whenever possible.

"It's my candy, and I can't give it away," Stevie replied, with a slight quiver in his voice.

"If you don't give it to me I'm gonna beat you up after school," threatened Vernon.

Those words will strike fear into the heart of any little kid. Nobody wanted to be on the receiving end of a "beat you up after school" threat. One, you would worry all day about the coming punishment, so much so that you could not concentrate on schoolwork. Two, if someone else heard the threat, the rumors would spread until all your classmates anticipated "the big fight." And three, to avoid the "beat you up meeting," you had to sneak out a different door and try to get home as fast as you could. This ran you the risk of being called a "chicken." Stevie didn't care if he got called chicken. That was fine and dandy! At least he'd be uninjured and safe at home, enjoying his Razzles!

Maybe, if I can get a message to Chucky, he'll walk me home and I'll escape the wrath of Vernon, Stevie pondered during class.

This was a problem, though, because Chucky was in the sixth grade, and all of the sixth grade classes were on the third floor. There was no way Stevie could find a way to get to the third floor without being noticed. Besides, he didn't know exactly where Chucky's class was located.

"Stephen, would you like to define that word for us?" Mrs. Lang, Stevie's third grade teacher, asked. She had a way of knowing by the distant look in her students' eyes who was not paying attention and she would call those students out.

"What's the word again?" Stevie asked as if he was listening, but just misunderstood the word.

"Ego," she restated.

"I don't know," Stevie confessed.

"You must pay attention Stephen. I just defined it while you were staring out the window. There will be a quiz on vocabulary tomorrow," she continued.

The last thing on Stevie's mind was a vocabulary quiz. He had more immediate concerns. A FIFTH-GRADER was going to beat him up after school! He might not even make it to the quiz, much less worry about the definition of "ego." It was already 2:30 pm;

school was out at 3:15 pm.

Maybe if I go home early with a stomach ache, I can get away? Stevie strategized briefly, but he knew he didn't want to lie to Mrs. Lang.

He watched the clock tick to 3:10 pm and he sighed. The bell would ring in only five minutes.

"OK class, put your chairs up and line up at the door," Mrs. Lang instructed. Normally Stevie was one of the last to leave, but not today. He cleared his desk, put his chair up, and was first in line at the door. Stevie was like a Kentucky Derby thoroughbred in the starting gate, waiting for the signal to race. His only option was to leave the classroom, go out the school's side door, then race home as fast as his legs could carry him. His heart was pounding, his mind was set, and his hand was in his pocket, gripping the Razzles.

Riiiiiiiinnnnnng!

The school bell rang. Stevie dashed out of the classroom.

"WALK, STEPHEN!" shouted Mrs. Lang sternly.

Stevie acted as if he didn't hear her. His life was at stake! To the side door he ran. He only had one block to go. One street stood between him and safety. Stevie usually walked down Slosson Street, but since Vernon lived in that direction, Stevie planned to go a different route. He slipped out the door and took the sidewalk toward Lawton Street, away from the school. He couldn't believe it! His plan was working! Until ...

POUND! Stevie felt a hand come down hard on

the back of his shoulder.

"Gimme dat candy boy!"

It was Vernon. Stevie jerked away from Vernon and took off running. Vernon gave chase and they covered the span of the front schoolyard. Stevie ran as hard as he could, with Vernon hot on his trail. All Stevie could think to do was to scream Chucky's name!

" C H U U U U C K K K K Y Y Y Y , CHUUUUCKKKKYYYY!" Stevie yelled, gasping for breaths between his shouts of distress.

Vernon was too fast for Stevie and his little third-grade legs. He caught Stevie in mid-stride and pushed him to the ground. Stevie's momentum forced him into a somersault. Vernon stood over him and proceeded to reach into Stevie's front right pocket, where the Razzles were tucked away. Vernon pulled them out, and they began a tug-of-war for possession of the Razzles. Suddenly, Chucky came from nowhere and, like an NFL linebacker making a game-saving tackle, knocked Vernon off of Stevie. The tackle was so swift, Vernon released his grip on the Razzles.

Now Chucky was sitting on top of Vernon! With one fearless, swift punch to Vernon's chest, Chucky settled the matter.

"Leave my brother alone!" Chucky commanded. "You mess with him again I'm gonna kick your butt!" It was a promise everyone knew Chucky would keep. (By the way, "I'm gonna kick your butt" is another one of those phrases you never want to hear.)

Chucky let Vernon up. Vernon took off for home in a slow, embarrassed trot. Stevie was relieved, but feared Vernon would go get his big brother and sic him on Chucky. His fears subsided when he recalled that he and Chucky had Raymond on their side. Nobody wanted to mess with one of the best athletes in the neighborhood, Raymond.

Stevie sighed, "Thank you Chucky. I was scared to death. Vernon wanted the Razzles I got in the cafeteria today. You want some?"

"That's all right Stevie," Chucky said. "Let's just go home."

Later that day, as he enjoyed his Razzles, Stevie thought about what happened. In reflection, he realized it probably would have been a good idea to simply tell Mrs. Lang that he had been threatened, but in his moment of fear Stevie didn't think of that. You need to know that if you are ever threatened, it's important to tell an authority figure. No one has the right to threaten you in physical, verbal, or psychological ways. Trusted grown-ups have solutions that children don't think about. If Mrs. Lang felt that Stevie was at risk, she may have let him stay for a little while after school to help her, then she would have ensured he got safely home. Decide ahead of time who you would go to if you are confronted by someone who threatens to hurt you, and you'll be better prepared.

The Adventures of Lil' Stevie

Too Much to Eat

Stevie had a difficult time trying to understand why his family was considered "poor." As far as he could see, they did pretty well. When he got home from school, there was always a snack waiting for him. Then, after a tough couple of hours playing outside, his mom always called him in for a good dinner. Lil' Stevie absolutely loved his mom's cooking. He would often hang out in the kitchen while Mom prepared dinner. Fried chicken days were among the best because of the delicious smell that lingered in the house all evening. His favorite side dishes were pork-n-beans, corn on the cob, applesauce, macaroni and cheese and, believe it or not, brussels sprouts. Sometimes Mom would fix pork chops, liver and onions, or fried fish. And even though Stevie loved Mom's fried chicken, his all-time favorite meal was her lasagna!

Another reason Stevie never understood why they were considered poor was because he always had decent clothes to wear. Being the baby of the family, he wore quite a bit of hand-me-downs. They didn't always look like hand-me-downs though because his mom would make minor adjustments to make them fit; like cuffing the pants or taking them in at the waist. If his clothes weren't hand-me-downs from his brothers or cousins, then they were certainly second-hand from either the Salvation Army Thrift Store, from garage sales, or, most often, from Goodwill. Lil' Stevie got new clothes on three occasions; Christmas, his birthday, and Easter! Stevie's family was not a regular church-going family, and Easter Sunday was considered THE day to go to church. You couldn't go to church on Easter unless you were dressed "clean" and that meant new clothes. Nope. Stevie's wardrobe certainly did not make him feel poor.

Stevie did notice that not everybody at his school used paper tickets to get their lunch each day the way he and Chucky did. Some students brought their lunch from home and others paid cash money for lunch. But Stevie never equated the meal tickets with being poor until someone told him.

"Your family must be poor," Bart said one day, as he and Stevie waited in the lunch line. Bart was a very smart classmate of Lil' Stevie's. He wore glasses, and, no matter how hot or cold it was outside, he always wore a button-up sweater.

"Why do you call us poor, Bart?" Stevie asked.

"My momma said that the kids with the paper meal tickets is on welfare. They can't afford to buy a lunch or pack a lunch from home," Bart responded. Stevie knew they were on welfare, but never understood the ins and outs or details of it all.

Bart's words didn't really matter much to Stevie. Sure, he could have been embarrassed, but welfare didn't hurt, and, as far as he knew, it was a good thing for him and his family. Being on welfare taught Stevie a lot about appreciating what you have.

For example, on the first of every month they received both food stamps and a welfare check. Food stamps were like pretty paper dollar bills. They could only be used for food at the store. Mom used the welfare money for the stuff they needed that food stamps couldn't buy; stuff like toilet paper, soap, and laundry detergent. It was exciting when the check and food stamps arrived. It meant there was money for grocery shopping. Stevie's mom did their full grocery shopping at the beginning of the month and the rest of the month she would only restock on essentials like milk, bread, cereal, and chip-chopped ham for sandwiches.

Stevie's job was very special on the big grocery shopping day. He had to keep the items in the cart separated. The things to be bought with food stamps had to be divided from the things to be bought with real money from the welfare check. Sometimes at the checkout Stevie's mom had more than she could pay for.

"Stevie!" she often called, while figuring prices in

her head. "Here honey, go put this big thing of aluminum foil back and get me the small one. Take this gallon of milk back too. Y'all only need one and you better make that last." Under her breath she'd usually murmur, "If y'all start turning off some of those lights around the house, we can cut that electric bill down and we won't be putting stuff back."

Sometimes Mom would go to one of Stevie's aunts' houses, who was also on welfare, and cut a deal. Although she really needed all the food stamps to feed her children, sometimes it was more important to keep the electricity on in the house. To do this, she would sell her food stamps to one of her sisters for cash to pay the bills. One time she desperately needed more cash to pay a bill, but didn't have any food stamps left to sell. All she had were Stevie's and Chucky's booklets of lunch meal tickets. She found a buyer, sold the lunch tickets, and paid the bill.

"Stevie and Chucky," she called to her sons, "come here, please!" Lil' Stevie and Chuck came into the kitchen and found their mom sitting at the kitchen table with bills and papers spread out in front of her. She smiled at them.

"This week we are going to do something different for lunch. You won't be eating at school, I will be fixing lunch for you," she said.

"Yeah!" Stevie said, knowing that any day Mom fixes lunch is a great day. Chucky knew something was wrong, but said nothing. He wasn't too fond of having to spend his entire lunchtime with his little brother. The boys left the kitchen and returned to the living room to watch their favorite Sunday-night television show.

Stevie stopped at the dining room and peeked back around the corner at his mom. The smile she'd given them had quickly faded. She buried her face in her hands, clasped her fingers together as if to pray, and slowly shook her head. Stevie tip-toed away, not wanting to be seen.

At lunchtime the next day, Chucky appeared quickly at Stevie's classroom door so they could walk home together. Stevie was excited for several reasons. First, it was always neat to be around Chucky! He was a great big brother. Second, it was weird to leave the school grounds in the middle of the day, but it was also fun, good exercise, and felt like an adventure. Best of all, Stevie looked forward to eating Mom's cooking. The boys ran all the way home. They wanted to eat quickly so they could return to school with at least a few minutes left of the lunch hour to enjoy the playground. When they came into the house, Stevie smelled oatmeal.

"Mom, you make the best oatmeal," Stevie swooned. He doctored it up with butter and sugar, then tore into his bowl.

"Slow down Stevie!" his mom chided. "Give that food a chance to get down to your belly."

Chucky wasn't very hungry, which left enough for Stevie to have seconds.

"Mom can I have some more?" Stevie asked hopefully.

"I guess so," Mom said with a sigh. Stevie scooped the rest of the oatmeal from the pot onto his plate. He swallowed every last spoonful and topped it off with a tall glass of milk.

"C'mon Stevie let's go! I wanna play on the playground before the bell rings," Chucky ordered. He was annoyed that Stevie's eating was cutting into his playtime.

The boys broke out of the house and began to run back to school.

"Chucky, can you slow down a little?" Stevie requested, out of breath.

"You gotta keep up Stevie. We are almost there," Chucky said. He was about 15 yards in front of Stevie, heading up the hill to Schumacher Elementary. Although it was a warm and sunny May day, Chucky was wearing a right-handed black leather glove he had found two days before. He wore that glove everywhere, as if it gave him super powers. But Stevie wasn't doing too well. He had eaten too much oatmeal and drank too much milk, in much too short of a time. His lunch had no time to settle before they started their run back to school. He could feel himself getting dizzy.

"CHUCKY!" Stevie shouted as he reached the corner.

He bent over, stabilizing himself with his hands on his knees. Chucky stopped running and turned back toward his brother. Just as Chucky made it to Stevie, it happened. Stevie threw up all of his oatmeal, butter, sugar, milk, and everything else he had in his stomach. Chucky instinctively STUCK HIS GLOVED HAND UNDER STEVIE'S MOUTH! Oatmeal covered Chucky's hand.

"What are you doing Chucky?" Stevie asked, when the retching ended.

"I dunno. I was trying to help," Chucky said in bewilderment.

The two boys realized, at the same time, how foolish Chucky's actions were. They burst out laughing. They laughed and laughed until their sides hurt.

"It's like I thought my glove was magic and could stop you from throwing up!" Chucky gasped.

"I was throwing up and the next thing I knew, when I looked down, I was staring into a big black glove covered with oatmeal," Stevie announced hysterically.

Lil' Stevie and Chucky continued on to school that day as if nothing happened. Stevie learned the importance of eating slowly and not eating too much. Although the food was good and he was very hungry, it's always best to do the wise thing. There is something to be said for being patient and not racing on to the next thing too soon.

It's still a mystery to Stevie how the bills stayed paid and the stomachs stayed full; especially when the money was gone and the month was far from over.

Stevie knows his mom was creative in finding solutions that would carry them through. It was oatmeal every day for lunch that week. Stevie didn't mind. Mom found a way to survive the tough times. No matter what problem you face in life, if you sit and think long and hard, there's probably an innovative solution that's waiting for you to show up. Then, when you have a good plan in place, everyone needs to know it and commit to following it. Even though Chucky wasn't thrilled with Mom's lunch plan, he did what the family needed him to do without complaining. When everyone works the plan, the plan works for everyone.

The Maneater

Grandma Eva was a master seamstress. She was Stevie's grandmother on his mother's side, and she could make anything. She was known throughout the family for her personalized quilts. All you had to do was bring her some of your favorite old clothes and, in a matter of days, she would present you with a quilt she made from them. She attached a tag to everything she made that read: "Made Especially For You By Eva Lee Walker."

Grandma Eva lived at 462 Livingston Street in a house that was set far off of the road. It had a long, narrow dirt driveway that seemed to Stevie to be about as long as a football field. In actuality, it was only about 40 yards long, but it had a large dirt area for parking that made it seem much bigger. She also had two gardens. Right in front of the house was a flower garden. Stevie was always careful passing the flower garden. Bees rested on Grandma Eva's flowers to get the sweet nectar from them. That garden wasn't big, but it had many different varieties of flowers that the bees loved. To the side of her house was a very large vegetable garden.

Stevie's Aunt Pearlie and her three sons lived with Grandma Eva. Frank was the oldest, then Billy. They both were about Chucky's age. Terry (whose real name was Phillip) was the youngest of the three. Terry and Stevie were the same age and were the best of friends.

Grandma Eva's house was the location for holiday celebrations, family get-togethers, and birthday parties. Many times Stevie and Chucky would sleep over with their cousins. Every visit was an adventure. Billy was good at everything and Frank was always creating something. One time, Frank made a real working bazooka! He cut the bottoms out of tin cans then taped them together, end to end, with black electrical tape. He stuffed a tennis ball in one end and a fuse in the other. He lit the fuse with the help of some lighter fluid and ... BOOM! The tennis ball exploded high into the air. Stevie was too young to play with the bazooka, but he knew Frank could maybe help him make a slingshot.

"Frank, can you show me how to make a slingshot?" Stevie asked hopefully. He suspected his mom might not totally approve, but he asked anyway.

"I don't know Stevie, you might put your eye out or something," Frank resisted.

"I won't hurt myself, or anybody else!" Stevie promised, pleading with his cousin.

"OK Stevie, just pay close attention. It's really easy. You're gonna need a wire coat hanger, an old tennis shoe and some rubber bands."

Stevie located the necessary supplies. Frank bent the wire hanger into a U-shape. He cut the tongue from the old shoe and made two holes, one at each end. He looped the rubber bands together, making two strings of three rubber bands. He took one string of rubber bands and attached one end of it to the hanger and the other through the hole on the tongue from the shoe.

He repeated it with the other string of rubber bands and, behold! Stevie had his own slingshot. Once Stevie had his slingshot, he, his cousins, and Chucky practiced shooting any chance they got. They never shot at people, just at cans and bottles they'd set up on an old brick wall. Of course, Billy was the best. But they all had fun trying.

In the big dirt yard at the front of the house they would play "Big Time Wrestling!" Chucky and Frank would draw a square wrestling ring in the dirt and they'd tag-team wrestle, just like the professionals. The winners would earn championship belts made from cardboard. The Akron Armory occasionally held Saturday Night Wrestling matches, but most of the boys' favorite wrestlers, like the ones they'd see on television, never made it to little Akron, Ohio. They wrestled in major cities, like Cleveland. Cleveland was too far away for them to ever get to go. Stevie's favorite was Big Cat Ernie Ladd. He played football for the

Kansas City Chiefs. The boys were also fans of Pampero Firpo, Abdullah the Butcher, and Crusher Verdu -- the man with a 63-inch chest!

"Chucky, Frank, Billy!" Aunt Pearlie called one day from the porch. She was interrupting a tag-team match that Chucky and Stevie were about to win.

"What, Ma?" Frank responded.

"Come here, boys!" she demanded. Stevie and Terry tagged along, even though they were not called. They were just being nosy.

"I just read in the paper there's going to be wrestling at the Armory Saturday night," she said. Stevie thought it was kind of weird that she stopped their championship match to tell them this. They already knew that the Armory had wrestling from time to time. They also knew that as a general rule they couldn't afford the ticket prices to go and watch.

"Who's wrestling, Mom?" Billy asked full of curiosity.

"I don't know," she said, trying to suppress her smile. "The paper said something about a Big Cat and Crusher 63 or something like that."

"BIG CAT ERNIE LADD!" Chucky and Frank shouted.

Then everyone said, "CRUSHER VERDU!" The boys were excited!

"Let me see, let me see the paper!" Billy demanded. Sure enough, The Big Cat Ernie Ladd, Pampero Firpo, and Crusher Verdu were all going to be in Akron, Ohio on Saturday night. Admission for children was $1.50. Aunt Pearlie's smile told them that the question was suddenly not whether or not they could go, but who was going to take them.

This would be Stevie's second time going to the Armory. The first time he went with his mom (and everybody else in Akron) to see James Brown, the Godfather of Soul. Stevie didn't think it was much fun, because he could barely see from their nose-bleed seats. But Big Time Wrestling was what Stevie loved and he'd sit anywhere in the building to see those guys. The week crept by at a snail's pace. Stevie couldn't remember he and his cousins ever anticipating something in Akron so much.

"We're going to drop you kids off at the Armory. When it's over, walk down to the All Night Grill and use the pay phone to call and we'll come pick you up," Aunt Pearlie instructed.

Stevie always liked Aunt Pearlie. Aunt Pearlie, like Stevie's mom, had to raise her kids alone. She was divorced too, but to make matters more difficult, Terry's dad was killed when Terry was in the first grade. Stevie was thankful that at least his dad was alive.

"Oh, another thing," she said to the older boys, "you boys stay together. Don't let Stevie and Terry get separated from you!"

They arrived early at the Akron Armory. The inside of the Armory was more intimidating than it was the last time Stevie was there. Maybe it was because the last time he was so far away from the concert stage. Today Chucky was going to make sure they were right on top of all the action. They ran to the lane where the wrestlers entered and exited the arena from the locker-room. It was blocked off, and Stevie saw Chucky reach out and slap Firpo on his sweaty arm as he walked by. Chucky had the boldness to do things Stevie would never dream of doing.

"I TOUCHED HIM, I TOUCHED HIM!" Chucky celebrated. "OOOOOH YEEEAHHH!"

Chucky roared, mimicking Pampero Firpo's signature growl. Chucky then turned to Stevie and Terry and threatened to wipe his sweaty hand on them. Stevie and Terry ran away in fear, not wanting to catch the "cooties." The boys ran all the way to ringside.

"Down in front!" shouted a patron who could no longer see the action because of where the boys stood.

"Keep it moving kids, unless you have tickets to be here," said the security guard.

They went to the first level and sat in the box seats until the usher made them move. That was the only time the boys sat the entire night. Pampero Firpo, the Argentinean Madman, wrestled first and won his match. That was followed by a few matches of no-name, unheard-ofs. They were obviously saving the main attraction for last.

Stevie began to feel sweaty.

"Terry, are you hot?" Stevie asked.

"No I'm not, but I see you are. You got sweat

dripping all over your head, Cousin," Terry noted.

"Yeah, I'm warm Terry, and I don't feel too good," Stevie confessed.

"In the red corner, hailing from Orange, Texas, formerly of the San Diego Chargers and the Kansas City Chiefs of the NFL … They call him The Big Cat … Let's hear some noise for Ernie Ladd!" the announcer declared from ringside. The place erupted.

"Oooouuuch!" Stevie said out loud.

"What's wrong, Stevie?" Terry asked.

"I don't know. It's my ear. It hurts every time the crowd cheers," Stevie winced. The pain was getting worse. Any increase in noise caused severe pain in Stevie's ear. At first it wasn't that bad, but now, in the middle of The Big Cat's match, it was horrible.

"Chucky!" Stevie shouted, trying to get Chucky's attention. He was almost in tears. "Chucky, Chucky! My ear hurts really bad."

"Awe Stevie … " Chucky said in disbelief, "how bad?"

"Really bad."

"Can you stay til wrestling is over?"

"I think I need to go to the hospital."

"THE HOSPITAL?" Chucky responded. "It's that bad?"

The announcer had just declared Ernie Ladd the winner. The crowd went crazy while the pain brought real tears to Stevie's eyes. Chucky knew he had to leave. Then Chucky realized *everyone* would have to leave, because they could not be separated. Chucky broke the news to Frank and Billy.

"Chuck are you SERIOUS?" Frank asked in disbelief. "Crusher Verdu is next!"

"Yep! He's crying real tears. He said he thinks he needs to go to the hospital," Chucky informed his cousins.

Stevie covered his right ear with one hand and wiped his tears with the other. He and Terry were already walking to the door. The big boys followed and soon they were all outside, behind the Armory, and on their way home. They headed to the All Night Grill to call for a ride. It was only four blocks straight down Main Street. The pain was not as bad outside. Still, Stevie kept his hand over his ear. He hadn't felt pain like that before. It was late on a Saturday night in downtown Akron, Ohio and most everything was closed except the Grill.

Chucky noticed that a man who came out of the Armory's back door around the same time they did was walking in the same direction, and he looked familiar.

"Hey Frank, I think that's Firpo!" Chucky whispered.

The older boys were excited at this thought, but Stevie and Terry were afraid. Pampero Firpo, the Argentinean Madman, was walking right in front of them!

"Let's follow him," Chucky suggested.

"No, Chucky!" Stevie pleaded. "Let's just go

home."

Stevie's protest landed on deaf ears. No way were his big cousins going to miss out on this once-in-a-lifetime opportunity. Firpo may have been a madman, but he was also a star. The big kids got their way. They began to follow one of the world's craziest men (other than the Butcher). Stevie and Terry tagged along reluctantly. It was creepy, and definitely scary. Young, defenseless boys, downtown, on a dark and deserted Akron night.

This is CRAZY! Stevie thought to himself.

"Where y'all think he's going?" Chucky asked. He made a right turn off of Main Street and walked right ... to the Holiday Inn Hotel.

He's not a maniac after all, Stevie thought. *He's just a man going to his hotel.*

"OK Chucky, he's just going to his hotel. Can't we go now?" Stevie begged trying to hide his fear. That wasn't good enough for Chucky.

"OOOOH YEEAAAAH," Chucky called in his deep, Pampero Firpo voice. The boys waited to see what the man would do.

"OOOOOOH YEEEAAAAHHH," Chucky called again, with more emphasis. Frank and Billy giggled.

Suddenly, the man stopped. The boys froze. Firpo quickly turned and faced the boys. He dropped his gym bag and sprinted full-speed, right at them! The pack of boys took off running, screaming at the top of their lungs. Stevie, Terry, Chucky, Frank, and Billy flew like the wind up Main Street.

"RUN, EVERYBODY!" Chucky encouraged. No one needed the prompting.

"HELP!" shouted Terry and Stevie as they ran ahead of the others. It was dark and there was absolutely no one on the streets.

Stevie ran so hard, either his ear was healed or he was too afraid to feel any pain. He pumped both arms as hard as he could. He was running for his life! He was certain he would be the only one caught and eaten by Pampero Firpo.

"We can stop, he's not even chasing us!" Billy suggested after they were at least two blocks away. They slowed a little.

"We gotta keep running until we are safe at the Grill! The man is crazy! He may have taken the side streets just to catch up with us," Frank said.

That scared Stevie even more. They resumed running. They ran all the way to the All Night Grill. They were completely out of breath when they arrived, but Stevie was relieved. They were safe. It felt like when you play tag and you get to home base where the person who is "It" can't get you. He was still a bit scared, but the fear turned into fun. It was quite a rush, sort of like the feeling you get on the first drop of a roller coaster ride. "You boys all right?" the owner asked in a slow country drawl. "You look like y'all seen a ghost."

"Yes sir, we're alright. We just need to use the

phone," Chucky explained. Frank had the change for the pay phone, Chucky was the spokesman, and Billy kept sticking his head outside to make sure no one was chasing them. Billy was right earlier. The "madman" never chased the boys; he just wanted them to think he was chasing them. He was comfortable in his hotel room by the time the boys got to the Grill.

Stevie's mom came to pick them up. She dropped Frank, Billy, and Terry at home before taking Chucky and Stevie to the emergency room at Akron General Hospital. Stevie was diagnosed with a severe ear infection. The doctor cleaned out Stevie's ears and gave him something for the pain. He gave Stevie's mom a prescription for medicine to make the infection go away. No Crusher Verdu that night. They didn't even get home until after two in the morning.

Things didn't go as the boys planned that night. Sometimes, things don't work out the way you expect them to either, do they? It's really nobody's fault. That's the way life is. But when you do things you shouldn't, like teasing people, then you may get just what you deserve. The boys got off easy after their encounter with Pampero, because he wasn't about to hurt them and no one got in trouble. Stevie realized though that it's always best to be where you are supposed to be, doing what you are supposed to be doing. Believe it or not, three weeks later Crusher Verdu was back in Akron. The boys were there, cheering him on. It was another great summer Saturday night in Akron, Ohio.

A Halloween Challenge

What kid doesn't like Halloween? Some people try to make Halloween all about ghosts, goblins, and ghouls, but for Lil' Stevie, Halloween is all about candy, candy, and more candy! Stevie knew all that scary stuff was fake and he had determined long ago never to be scared of it. All he could think about was the candy.

Lil' Stevie had a younger cousin named Dino. Dino was an only child, the son of his mom's baby sister, Aunt Sarah. On special occasions, like Halloween, Dino often shared the fun with Lil' Stevie's family. Halloween was one of Stevie's favorites. Most years, Stevie, Chucky, and Dino would dress up in creative homemade costumes. They'd make themselves a Native American Indian, or put a sheet over their head and go as a ghost. But one year, Dino had one of those store-bought costumes like many of the other kids wore. He was Casper the Friendly Ghost.

Stevie's mother wouldn't let them go too far away from the house for trick-or-treating. She had heard terrifying stories of bad things that happened to kids who were out late on Halloween and tales of candy-tampering that made her worry for her kids' safety.

For example, there was the one time that someone reported finding a razor blade in an apple. A kid bit into it and cut his mouth. There was another report of a student becoming sick after eating some homemade cookies from his Halloween bag. The cookies were tainted with drugs! With these stories circulating the mom-circuit, Ms. Fitzhugh laid down some hard-core trick-or-treating rules for the Fitzhugh boys and Dino. There was to be NO EATING ANY CANDY until it was inspected by their mother. The first thing Lil' Stevie's mom did was throw away everything in the trick-or-treat bags that was unwrapped.

"Awe ... Mom!!!" Stevie moaned. He and Dino had stopped home to dump their candy bags so they could go out and reload. Mom had begun sorting through it all and taking out the suspicious pieces. "That candy is OK, the wrapper must've come off in the bag."

"Nope. I'm sorry son, it's got to go. You know the rule. No unwrapped candy, no fruit, and nothing that we can't identify," Stevie's mom said without regret.

"Look at all of that candy we gotta throw away, cousin Stevie ... " Dino said slowly in disbelief, shaking his head.

"C'mon, Dino. We need to hurry up and head back out there before it gets dark," Stevie insisted.

"Don't go too far, boys. Those street lights better not come on before you get back!"

The kids had to be home before dark. That was a rule that was in effect year-round, not just on Halloween. So there was no dispute as to when "dark" was, the streetlights were used as the guide. If the streetlights were on, then it was dark and you'd better be home. Stevie learned that lesson the hard way.

One night, Stevie was down the block playing with his friends Crystal, Wendy, and Monica, the Stark girls. Crystal was Stevie's age, Wendy was a little bit younger, and Monica was the youngest. When the streetlights came on, Stevie ignored them. Stevie figured since his mom didn't call him in maybe it was OK to stay out longer.

Ring-a-ling-a-ling! Stevie's home phone rang. It was Mrs. Dandridge calling. She lived just two doors down from the Fitzhugh's and directly across the street from the Starks.

"Hello?" Stevie's mom answered the phone.

"Eva? This is Mrs. Dandridge down the street. I see Stevie down here playing and I know these streetlights been on for a little while now," she reported.

Mrs. Dandridge would not only report you, but she felt she had the right to spank you if you needed it. She was the lady that knew everybody's business on the block. Sometimes she would just sit on her porch, watch, and listen.

"Thank you Mrs. Dandridge, I'll call him in," Stevie's mom promised, somewhat amused. Even so, Stevie got a good little spanking that night!

So he knew his mom was serious when she said be home before the streetlights came on. He and Dino rushed out the house in their costumes for the last round of trick-or-treating for this Halloween. They hadn't yet covered the houses on Slosson Street to Greenwood Avenue. The candy started coming again, fast and heavy.

"We hit the jackpot!" Dino said to Stevie.

It seemed like every house on the block was participating. When Stevie looked down at the row of houses almost every porch light was on and very few kids were still out. A lit porch light was a beautiful thing to see because it meant that treats were available at that house. Door to door Stevie went with Dino following behind. Candy, candy, and more candy. It was just starting to get dark when Stevie saw Chucky coming their way.

"Chucky!" Stevie called. "Look at all the candy we got!"

Chucky didn't seem all that impressed. His own bag had just as much as Stevie's and Dino's put together.

"Where did you get all of that candy Chucky?" Stevie asked, a bit jealous, but also proud of his big brother. He was the man.

"I move fast, Stevie. C'mon y'all, let's head home, it's starting to get dark," Chucky said.

"One more house Chucky, please!" Stevie asked.

"No, Stevie I went to that house and you don't wanna go there," Chucky warned.

"Why not? They got their light on!" Stevie pressed.

"OK, man, I've been up there already. I'll wait for y'all. Just hurry up," Chucky said, fighting back a sly smile.

Stevie and Dino ran up to the house. It was the last one. A big tree in the front yard really made it spooky. Stevie rang the bell. An old man opened the door and held out a basket of tootsie rolls. Dino grabbed a handful first. As soon as Stevie reached for his, a ten-foot tall monster leapt from the bushes!

"ROOAAARRR!" screamed the hairy monster.

Stevie and Dino bolted off the porch. Stevie ran over top of poor Dino as they headed to the sidewalk and back to Chucky, who was doubled over with laughter. Stevie and Dino, with hearts still racing from the adrenaline rush of the scare, joined Chucky and they all had a good laugh.

The "monster" was nothing more than somebody in a cheap Bigfoot costume. It was a good scare though, and another great memory.

With darkness quickly approaching, the boys headed back down Slosson Avenue. Another Halloween had come and gone. Stevie and Dino continued to rehearse their frightened response to the monster at the last house. As they walked, Chucky noticed a black kickball about thirty yards down the block. Chucky quickly made a wager.

"Hey Stevie, I bet I can kick that ball all the way down to Hawkins," Chucky boasted.

Just down the hill from Roslyn Avenue (Chucky and Stevie's street) was Orlando Avenue, and the busy street after that was Hawkins Avenue. Chucky was always trying to outdo everybody in everything. He always wanted to prove that he could throw farther, run fastest, jump the highest, and, this day, kick the ball the hardest.

"No way, Chucky!" Stevie defied. "There's no way you can kick that ball all the way down to Hawkins."

Since it was downhill all the way, it actually was possible that with a good kick and a generous roll, Chucky could boot that ball all the way to Hawkins.

"He can do it Stevie," Dino said. "Chucky can do anything!"

"OK, Stevie. If the ball goes all the way to Hawkins, then I can get a handful of your candy. If not, then you can get a handful of my candy," Chucky posed.

"Deal!" Lil' Stevie agreed.

Chucky was now about twenty feet away from the black kickball. Chucky raised his arms as if to quiet the crowd. He eyed the ball and lined up his approach.

"You can do it, cousin Chucky! Kick it hard! Kick it HAAARRRDDDD!" Dino cheered.

Chucky was now ten feet away. He began his approach. Stevie had his fingers crossed. Stevie REALLY wanted some of Chucky's candy. Chucky moved faster now, and was almost ready to kick, like a NFL field goal kicker. Chucky stepped perfectly at the ball, planted his left foot, and, with all of his might, drew back his right foot and launched it firmly into the ball.

"OOOOOOOOOOUUUUCHHHH! OW ... OW ... OW!" Chucky hopped on one foot, holding the other, then fell to the ground in pain. The ball moved about five feet. It wasn't a kickball, it was a BOWLING BALL!

"You OK, Chucky?" Stevie asked, fighting back giggles.

"Ouch! My foot, my FOOOOOT!" Chucky repeated. He got up and began to walk off the pain. When Stevie and Dino saw that Chucky wasn't seriously hurt, they let loose their laughter.

"AHHHH HHHHHAAA!" Stevie blurted. "The ball didn't even move!"

"It's not funny!" shouted Chucky. "I almost broke my foot!"

"It was funny to me, seeing you hopping around like a kangaroo!" Stevie said. Chucky had to admit, it was kind of funny.

"A bowling ball," Chucky said. "Who left a

bowling ball out here?"

The ball was so heavy, Chucky couldn't even pick it up to roll it. They just left it there. Chucky found himself in a lot of pain, and walked with a limp all the way home. Stevie made sure Chucky's candy bag was *much* lighter. He two-fisted his reward for winning the bet by grabbing as much candy as he could from Chucky's bag. It was a sweet Halloween. Literally.

Chucky made up his mind to kick what he thought was a kickball. Unfortunately, he didn't have all of the information. Sometimes we regret things we say or do because we act without having all of the information. Remember to get all of the information, hear the whole story, and know the whole truth before you say or do something that ends up causing you pain or hurts a friend.

Grandma's Secret

Lil' Stevie was fortunate. Not all little boys and girls grow up with both of their grandmothers nearby. Grandma Angeline, Stevie's father's mom, spoiled Lil' Stevie by treating him special. She called him her "baby's baby."

Grandma Eva was Stevie's mom's mom (Stevie's mom was also named Eva). Stevie was closer to Grandma Eva, largely because his first cousin and best friend Terry, along with Terry's brothers, lived with her. Grandma Eva had a large amount of Native American blood in her lineage. Her complexion was light reddish brown, and her facial features had distinct Cherokee characteristics. She normally wore her long black hair up in a bun. Often at night Lil' Stevie would enjoy sitting with his grandmother as she brushed her hair. When let down, her hair easily came down past her shoulders. It was beautiful.

"Can I touch your hair, Grandma?" Stevie often

asked.

"Sure baby, you know you can touch Grandma's hair," she always responded.

Then she'd give him a great big gummy smile. Grandma Eva wore dentures, but she normally never put them in unless they were having company or if she was going out of the house to church or somewhere special. Stevie would run his fingers through Grandma Eva's beautiful long hair as often as he could.

If Stevie had to pick one thing he *didn't* like about Grandma Eva, it was that she dipped snuff and chewed Redman Chewing Tobacco. When she chewed tobacco she always had to spit. That was nasty. But other than that, Stevie hung out with Grandma Eva as much as he could. Grandpa Seaborn, her husband, died of cancer just a few months before Stevie was born, so Stevie only knew him through the stories people told. When Stevie would see Grandma Eva dip, he'd remember hearing that Grandpa Seaborn smoked unfiltered Camel cigarettes.

Stevie learned so much stuff when he was with his grandmother. When Grandma spoke, school was in session.

"Grandma, how come your garden is always so good?" Stevie asked one day, while working the garden with Grandma.

She had rows and rows of corn that grew much taller than Lil' Stevie. She had big ripe tomatoes, greens, green beans, snap peas, carrots, squash, and many other kinds of vegetables. Stevie sometimes stayed with Grandma the entire morning in the garden. They pruned, picked, and shared TLC with the vegetables. Stevie's cousins slept almost until noon, but Stevie was an early riser like Grandma. Stevie could never beat Grandma to waking up though. He didn't mind because when he did get up, she would cook him breakfast.

"You gotta give your garden a lot of TLC," Grandma said, in reply to Stevie's question.

"What's TLC?" Stevie asked.

"Oh, baby, T-L-C is Tender, Loving, Care. You cain't just treat your garden any kind of way. You gotta care for it, be sweet to it, and treat it with dignity. People are the same way, baby. You cain't just mistreat people and expect them to act right towards you. When you grow up Stevie, make sure you treat people right and in the end they gonna treat you right, back."

"That's why your garden grows so big and strong and pretty? Because you give it TLC?" Stevie suggested.

"That's right Steeb, you show'nuff learnin' now boy," Grandma said.

When she didn't have her teeth in, she had a hard time pronouncing her 'v's. So *Steve* ended up sounding like *Steeb*. By noon the sun was in full effect. Stevie followed Grandma back into the house. Grandma washed the freshly picked vegetables, cut them up, and made a special batch of what she called Cha-cha. Cha-

cha was a special vegetable spread she made that was put on greens. It was "De-Lish!" as Stevie would say. She would can it in special mason jars and pass them out to the family.

Often times Lil' Stevie took the opportunity during his special Grandma-time to get his questions about life answered. Grandma always had an answer, even for Stevie's toughest questions.

"Grandma, why do people who say they love each other still fight and separate?" Stevie asked as Grandma was working on her Cha-cha. Stevie still struggled with his parents' divorce.

"Just like my garden needs the right ingredients to grow, so do people. My plants need sunshine, good soil, and oxygen. That's the right enbironment. It's the same in a family. You have to have the right enbironment. The enbironment is all the things the family needs to grow. A family needs lub, forgibeness and fafe. There's gotta be plenty lub 'cause sometimes people are hard to lub. You need forgibeness because sometimes we say things and do things that hurt others. We don't wanna hurt anybody, but we do, so we need forgibeness. And a family needs fafe. Fafe is how you hope for things to be better one day. You believe so strong that it's gonna be better that it becomes hope. Hope will neber let you down."

"That's environment, Grandma?" Stevie asked. "Love, forgiveness, and faith?"

"It's the right kind of enbironment, Baby,"

76

Grandma said. "Without the right enbironment, it's pain and misunderstanding all the time."

"You're so smart, Grandma," Stevie said.

"Oh, it's not smart, Baby, it's wisdom," Grandma said. "After all these years of libin', I learned a thing or two. There aren't really many problems in life, just decisions that need to be made. Besides, I gotta secret that gibbs me a little edge."

Stevie perked up even more. A secret!

There's something about knowing a secret that makes you feel special, Stevie thought.

"A secret!" Stevie said.

"Yes, Baby, a secret," Grandma replied.

"You gonna tell me, Grandma?" Stevie asked, with expectation.

"One day sugah, one day when you a wee bit olda."

"I'm old enough now, Grandma. I can keep your secret."

"It's not a secret to keep, it's secret to use," Grandma corrected Stevie.

"If it's a secret to use, then can you let me use it now? I wanna be wise like you!" Lil' Stevie continued. But Grandma just chuckled and shook her head.

The more Stevie talked about Grandma's secret, the more he wanted to know it and use it. He began to think about Grandma's wisdom. Grandma had answers for everything. Stevie brought all of his concerns to Grandma. And no matter what it was, Grandma spoke wisdom to it.

If I can know the secret now, when I'm young, by the time I get old I could probably be one of the wisest and smartest persons around, Stevie thought to himself. *If I knew Grandma's secret I could get the best grades, make the best decisions, and everyone would think of me as the one with all the answers.*

Stevie was so consumed by Grandma's secret that he even dreamed about it that night. In his dream he was a famous explorer who was set on the task of discovering "Grandma's Secret."

The scene was tropical waters surrounding a small chain of islands, much like Hawaii. Lil' Stevie set sail for the uninhabited Island of Faraway Dreams. His small sailboat approached the sandy shores of the tiny island. Legend had it that no boat ever touched the shores and no traveler ever survived the short journey to the center of the island where Grandma's Secret was located. Sure enough, Stevie's small vessel became firmly lodged in the deep coral reef just beyond the shoreline.

Stevie grabbed his knife, determined to continue his journey by swimming the rest of the way to the shore. As Stevie dove into the warm waters, fears filled his head with tall tales of sea creatures prowling the waters to protect Grandma's Secret from intruders.

Stroke by slow, tiring stroke, Stevie swam his way to the island shore. What once seemed a lifetime away was now closer and closer. He occasionally felt the slight brush of schools of fish against his bare legs. He tried not to think of the fabled man-eating sea monsters lurking about. He was almost to the shore when, without warning, he felt a long prickly hand grab his right ankle.

"AHHHHHH!" Stevie let out an ear-piercing scream. Convinced he was going under, he yanked free with one hard kick. It was not a sea creature after all, just seaweed that swirled around his leg as he entered the shallow water. Although his life was not in danger, it gave him quite a fright.

An exhausted Stevie made it to the shore. He lay on the beach in the hot sand as the warm sun dried his body. He rolled to his back to catch his breath.

"I am almost there," he mumbled aloud. "Soon I'll know Grandma's Secret!"

His knife, which was large enough to pass as a sword, was still strapped to his side. He gathered his strength and continued to the center of the island, where Grandma's Secret was rumored to be hidden. Men from all over the world had attempted to discover Grandma's Secret on this remote island. None had gotten as far as Stevie. Proud of his progress, Stevie left the beach and marched forward. The bush was so thick he used his knife to clear the path in front of him. His muscles ached as the once warm and friendly sun now burned intensely from above, launching the temperature into the danger zone. Stevie persisted. Sweat stung his eyes as he imagined the success of acquiring Grandma's

Secret.

Chop, chop, Chop! Stevie cut away the bush that slowed his progress.

"Ya-ya, ya-ya, whooo-heee!" Stevie heard an unrecognizable language faintly in the distance.

"I thought this island was uninhabited," Stevie said aloud to himself. Stevie swung his knife stronger, harder, and faster. "Maybe the voices are friendlies or natives committed to preserve the safety of Grandma's Secret?"

Either way, time was running out. The voices were getting closer.

Will they have poisonous darts, will they burn me as a sacrifice, will they throw me over the cliff? Terrible, fearful thoughts raced through Stevie's head.

Just as he felt he could go no further, a clearing appeared. As the trees and the bush thinned out, he no longer needed his knife to clear the path. He began to run faster and faster.

"Ya-ya, ya-ya, whooo-heee! Ya-ya, ya-ya, whooo-heee!" The voices seemed to be upon him. He began to sprint through the open space.

"This has to be the center of the island," Stevie declared. "Where's Grandma's Secret?"

Just then the island natives made it to the clearing. Tribal paint streaked their faces in bright colors. They raised their warrior weapons high in hot pursuit of the uninvited guest.

Stevie ran for his life. In the distance he saw what

looked to be a treasure chest. It was awkward to run with his large knife in his hand, so he dropped it. The increase in speed helped him pull away from the natives. He made a beeline for the chest. It was indeed a beautiful treasure chest. The words *Grandma's Secret* adorned the lid in letters made from diamonds.

The sun was setting. His heart pumped with electric fear. All he had to do was open the chest, get the secret, and hide in the bush as darkness came. Under the cover of darkness, he could retrace his steps to the shore to return to his boat.

"Oh no!" Stevie cried. "This can't be!"

The chest wouldn't open! There was no lock, it just wouldn't open! Stevie tried and tried.

Ssssffffooot! An arrow stuck in the ground behind him. *Ssssffffooot!* Another arrow, then another, each closer than the last. The natives were getting nearer.

"Ya-ya, ya-ya, whooo-heee! Ya-ya, ya-ya, whooo-heee!"

Fearing for his life, Stevie gave the chest one last shake. He turned it on its side to get the secret to come out. Nothing happened.

Ssssffffooot! Another arrow landed, this time at Stevie's foot. He turned with desperation in his eyes and saw three more arrows already in the air. There was no escape. His heart sunk. The mission failed. Stevie watched, as if in slow motion, as the three fateful arrows dropped from the sky.

"GRANDMAAAAAA!" Stevie yelled an instant

before the arrows met his skin.

"STEEB, STEEB ... Steebie, wake up boy!" Stevie opened his eyes. Grandma was standing over him. "Boy, why was you screamin' for me like that? You musta been habin' a bad dream or sumptin'."

"I dreamed I was on a voyage to find your secret," Stevie said.

"I guess my secret is gonna worry you to death, Boy. I might as well go ahead and tell you so you won't die of a heart attack from habin' nightmares," Grandma said with a faint chuckle through her toothless grin.

"You gonna tell me your secret, Grandma?" Stevie said as he sat up in the bed.

"My secret, Baby, is simple. For as long as I can remember I been using this secret. I call it seben and eleben."

"That's it?" Stevie said in disbelief. "Seven and eleven? I don't get it, Grandma. What does that mean? How do you get wisdom from that?"

"I reads my Bible twice-a-day, everyday, at seben in the morning and eleben o'clock at night. That's how I gets my wisdom. The Bible is full of wisdom, and I tries to get as much as I can."

Stevie learned the real meaning of education from Grandma. Education doesn't only come from what the teachers teach, but it also depends on what the students seek to learn. The most important way to learn includes reading. For Grandma Eva, it was reading her Bible every day. Stevie wasn't quite ready for that yet, but for now he did begin to read and read and read until he was ready to read what Grandma read. Stevie didn't read only at 7 and 11, he read after school, in the evening, on Saturdays, and on Sundays. He did this because he wanted to obtain wisdom. When you want something bad enough, you'll do whatever you must to make it happen. Lil' Stevie did become smarter, his grades were better, and school became easier as a result of his commitment to read.

The Adventures of Lil' Stevie

A Need for Speed

Lil' Stevie spent about half of his summer nights at his grandma's house. Not just because she was one of his favorite people (she really was), but because his cousin Terry, who was the same age as Stevie and was his best friend, lived with Grandma Eva. From the time Stevie and Terry woke up and had their Cocoa Puffs cereal until the sun was down and they were inside the house for the night, it was all play.

When it was really hot they'd go swimming. They didn't swim the way most kids went swimming. There was a small park, no bigger than one square block, just beyond Akron General Hospital. It had lots of grassy areas and a few benches, but the main attraction was the fountain. It had a small cement center with a spout that spewed water straight into the air. A circular trough caught the water from the spout. It was about two feet deep, which wasn't much, but it was the perfect swimming spot for Stevie and his cousins.

The boys didn't have swimsuits. Whatever cut-off shorts they had on that day became their swimwear. They removed their socks and shoes, pulled off their shirts, and they were ready to take the plunge. They called it swimming, but it was more like splashing. It wasn't really deep enough to put their faces under, and besides, none of them could actually swim.

Just like they had to be creative with their swimming, Stevie and Terry had to be creative with their playing. They didn't have bikes or neat toys like the other kids had, so some days they would cross the street to play with the Decatur children. Richard Decatur, better known as Pookie, was the oldest. John-John was his little brother. They had the best toys! They had REAL Tonka Trucks (not the fake kind that just looked like real Tonka, but broke after the first time you played with them). They also had a basketball hoop that was made just for small kids.

One day, after playing with Pookie and John-John, Terry suggested they go down to the park where there was a big, regular-sized basketball hoop.

"Let's go down the street Stevie, and see what the big boys are doing at Sam's Court," Terry suggested.

"That's a good idea Terry," Stevie replied.

Terry and Stevie said goodbye to the Decatur boys and headed down Livingston Street. Sam's Court was hoppin' with activity and the boys played with their friends all afternoon. By the time they headed home, they were good and tired.

The boys crossed the street and headed towards Grandma's house. Shortly after they crossed, they realized they had a big problem. They forgot about the dogs! There were two medium-sized dogs to watch out for on this side of the street. One was a loose, wild dog that didn't belong to anyone in particular. This dog would chase you, but would run away if you chased it back. The other dog was named Blackie. Blackie belonged to Ms. Williams, who lived right next door to Stevie's grandmother. Ms. Williams' house was much closer to the road than Grandma's because of Grandma's long driveway and big front yard.

"What do we do, Stevie?" Terry asked as their predicament became clear.

"I dunno," Stevie replied. "We can't break the rule."

"The Rule" was they could only cross the street back and forth one time while they were out playing. They had already crossed once to play with the Decaturs and then crossed back over after they went to Sam's Court. So now they had to stay put. Stevie wished they had remembered about the dogs sooner. Now, Blackie would probably chase them forever and maybe even bite them.

"Woof, woof, woof!" Blackie sounded off from Ms. Williams' porch as the boys approached.

"What now?" Stevie asked. They had to pass Blackie's porch to get home. They just couldn't go back across the street to get around Blackie without permission.

"We might as well keep going. If we don't run, maybe Blackie won't chase us," Terry responded.

"But what if he does? What will we do?" Stevie said to Terry with a slight bit of fear in his voice.

"We'll just go real slow," Terry suggested. "If Blackie does chase us, we'll run as fast as we can."

"I don't know about this, Terry."

"We can do it, Stevie."

"What if he catches us, Terry?"

"Don't even think about that, Stevie. He won't catch us."

The boys slowly approached Ms. Williams' house. Blackie increased the intensity of his barking, becoming more and more agitated. Stevie and Terry tried not to look in Blackie's direction. Stevie especially didn't look it in the eyes. Chucky always said that staring into a dog's eyes only makes it angrier. They reached Ms. Williams' house. Stevie took a quick peek at the porch.

"Yep!" Stevie said. "Blackie is definitely off of his leash."

"Don't stare at him, Stevie, just keep walking," Terry said coolly.

They successfully passed Ms. Williams' house. Standing now at Grandma's driveway, they were almost safely home. Blackie was still barking, but it seemed as if he was going to give the boys a break today. Both Stevie and Terry breathed a sigh of relief but before they were even through exhaling, Blackie leapt from his porch and, with lightning speed, headed toward the boys.

"RUN!" Terry shouted. Stevie and Terry bolted down Grandma's driveway as if competing in the Olympic 100-meter dash. Blackie was close behind.

"Don't look back, Stevie, just go, go, GO!" Terry hollered.

Stevie and Terry raced all the way down the driveway. It seemed longer than ever!

"WOOF, WOOF, WOOF!" Blackie threatened. Every gallop brought him closer. The boys approached Grandma's porch and, with one gigantic leap, in the nick of time, jumped up and over the steps and landed safely on the porch. They were just beyond Blackie's reach. He came to a dusty halt in the dirt at the bottom of Grandma's porch stairs. As soon as he stopped, Blackie turned and retreated. He hastily ran back up the driveway and returned to the comfort of his own porch.

"Wooo-weee! THAT was close!" Stevie said. "Blackie almost had us!" The boys were both relieved and thrilled by the chase.

"I was scared, but that was fun," Stevie confessed between breaths. Terry could only manage a nod. He was completely out of breath. As far as activity for a late summer afternoon, the chase ranked right up there with an amusement park ride on the exhilaration scale. Stevie had an idea.

"Hey Terry, let's do it again."

"Are you crazy?" Terry asked. "We barely made it!"

Stevie was just a little taller than his cousin Terry. The longer legs gave Stevie a small advantage, but both of the boys were fast. VERY fast.

"If we get a head start, Blackie will never catch us!" Stevie proposed. "Besides, Blackie has to work harder than both of us. His legs are small!"

"Yeah, but he's got four legs and we only have two legs," Terry observed.

"But Terry, you KNOW that was fun!" Stevie continued. "Let's do it just one more time! I bet you can't beat me!"

"I bet I can," Terry retorted.

The two boys set out. When they got near the street they each had secret second thoughts, but neither wanted to back out now.

"You scared?" Terry asked.

"I'm not scared. You scared, Terry?"

"Naw, man, I'm not scared."

They reached the street. Blackie was resting peacefully on his porch. Stevie knew the slightest noise would get his attention because he was a nosy dog. Stevie threw a stick onto the sidewalk near Ms. Williams' house. Sure enough, Blackie looked up. Race number two was on.

"RUN!" the boys shouted in unison.

They dashed down the driveway with all of their might, just as before. And, like the first time, they barely escaped from Blackie, who chased them all the way to the porch. It was fun. In fact, it was so much fun they did it a third time, a fourth time, and even a fifth time.

Each time the boys narrowly escaped by jumping onto the porch. The day was almost done. Running from Blackie was a grueling workout. Grandma sat in her rocking chair, mending clothes with a needle and thread. With the front door open, she watched every "Blackie versus the Boys" episode with amusement.

Those silly boys gonna sleep good tonight, she thought to herself with a smile.

Stevie and Terry were about to come inside. It was starting to get dark. In fact, it was getting harder and harder to see Blackie. (He was named Blackie for a reason.)

"Last time Terry, let this be the last time," Stevie requested.

"You go ahead, Stevie."

"I'm not gonna do this by myself, Terry. C'mon, do it with me. Just this last time, then we can go inside," Stevie begged.

"Alright, one last time," Terry surrendered.

The boys did the same thing they'd been doing. They made it to the top of the driveway's slight hill. Livingston Street was emptied of any pedestrians, as most folks had gone indoors. Even the Decaturs across the street were inside. You could still see some of their toys that they left out. The boys strained to make out

Blackie's form on Ms. Williams' porch.

"Do you see him, Stevie?"

"No I don't, Terry, let's get closer."

The boys tiptoed a step or two closer to Ms. Williams' porch. There was no Blackie. The boys didn't know it, but Blackie went on an adventure of his own, chasing another dog in the opposite direction. Blackie had a surprise in store for the boys. Blackie noticed the boys near his yard and came strolling up behind them.

"WOOF, WOOF, WOOF!" Blackie charged. Blackie startled the boys so much, all they had time to do was turn and run. They were completely caught off-guard. They ran back to Grandma's driveway from one direction, and Blackie ran to the driveway from the other. They had to beat Blackie to the driveway and outrun him to the porch.

"RUN STEVIE!" Terry shouted.

Because it was dark, each stride was a risk. Footing was unsure. The boys ran as fast as they could toward the house. Blackie was right on their heels, closer than ever before. The porch came into view. Blackie barked ferociously. Stevie and Terry ran for their lives, while Grandma chuckled from inside the house. With one final burst of energy from their weary legs, Stevie and Terry barely managed to clear the stairs and land on the porch. Once again, they escaped Blackie, or did they?

The boys arrived safely on the porch, but Blackie did something he hadn't done all day. BLACKIE

JUMPED UP ONTO THE PORCH, RIGHT BEHIND THE BOYS! Blackie had never come up on Grandma's porch before. The boys nearly went into cardiac arrest! Blackie had them cornered!

"GRANDMA!" the boys screamed in unison at the top of their lungs.

Not knowing what to do, the boys stood there, panicked and panting, backing away from Blackie. Blackie enforced his "win" with a few more barks and a growl. Then Blackie left.

"Git on 'way from heah!" Grandma yelled at Blackie through her gums. She wore a big ol' grin. She couldn't hide her laughter as her grandbabies called her name in their moment of fear.

"You boys know bettah than t'be messin' wit dat dawg," she chided.

Grandma saved the day. Blackie ran all the way home. The boys hugged Grandma. With one on each hip, Grandma hugged back. They thanked their grandma for getting rid of Blackie.

Sometimes, if you do something you shouldn't, and you don't get caught, you'll be tempted to continue to do it again and again. You might begin to think you can get away with whatever you want! One of the biggest myths people believe is that they can do whatever suits them, and there will never be consequences. The truth is, the consequences of wrong will always catch you some way or some how. If it doesn't catch up with you today, then probably tomorrow. If not tomorrow, then you can be sure that when you least expect it, you'll have to face the consequences.

Lil' Stevie learned many life lessons growing up in Akron, Ohio. Life continues to be an adventure for Lil' Stevie, even though now he is older. As you travel through the adventures of your life, remember to be thankful for every day, because every day is a treasure.

THE END